NEVER MIND THE HOOPS

THE **HOOPS**

The Ultimate CELTIC

QUIZ BOOK

DAVID POTTER

The
History
Press

First published 2014

The History Press
The Mill, Brimscombe Port
Stroud, Gloucestershire, GL5 2QG
www.thehistorypress.co.uk

British Library Cataloguing in Publication Data.
A catalogue record for this book is available from the British Library.

ISBN 978 0 7509 5223 1

Typesetting and origination by The History Press
Printed in Great Britain

Contents

Introduction

Celtic are a team of legend with a rich history. From humble origins they have grown to become the huge worldwide concern which they are today. Great men have done great things for the club and the end product has always been (or at least attempts to be) good football, played with an emphasis on attacking, the desire to win but the desire to entertain as well. I once had a discussion with a Celtic manager and a Lisbon Lion about which was the more important – winning or entertaining – but to a large extent, this debate is a bogey, because Celtic have traditionally attempted (they haven't always succeeded!) to do both simultaneously.

This perhaps explains why they attract such love and devotion from their great number of supporters – an enthusiastic fan base which in worldwide terms is possibly the largest of them all. Some are Celtic supporters for ethnic reasons (no point in denying that) but a greater and now ever-increasing number are attracted to the club because of what they stand for. As well as good football, there is a commitment to charitable causes – the Thai Tims, Jimmy Johnstone's Motor Neurone charity, the 125 Charity and so on – which dates back from the earliest of times, and a broad-based selection policy which has guaranteed that the team is supported by people of all religions and of none.

But how much do their supporters really know about the club? Probably a great deal more than supporters of other clubs know about theirs, for Celtic have always been rich in the amount of books, videos, DVDs, ephemera and souvenirs that one can find. Wisely the club have done a great deal to encourage this, for the old adage is surely true, stating that 'he who is not interested in his past, has no future'.

This book is in no sense a 'heavy' book. It can be picked up and put down whenever one wants. It is both for the eclectic reader and the serious historian, and it is to be hoped that lovers of other clubs (who must always be respected and made welcome by Celtic supporters) will pick up this book and learn a little more about this great organisation to which so many people are in (voluntary) emotional thraldom.

There are 30 rounds of 12 questions each. Deliberately the answers are on different pages, so that you cannot cheat (well, you can of course but you are just kidding yourself and not anybody else!), and the questions vary in difficulty. I would like to think that there will be some supporters who can get 360 answers right out of 360, but anyone who gets 300 at his or her first attempt really does know a great deal about Celtic. The book of course can be used for groups and even for quiz functions, and what a wonderful way of passing the time in the minibus on the long journeys to Aberdeen, Inverness and Ross County!

Enjoy, and keep on loving the Celtic!

David Potter,
April 2014

Round 1

All the Macs

For a team that plays in Scotland and attracts fans from both Scotland and Ireland, it is hardly surprising that Celtic have lots of Mcs and Macs. Spelling of Mc and Mac can be confusing and apologies to anyone whose name we have misspelled.

1   In the 1911 Scottish Cup final, Celtic had a McAtee and McAteer (Christian names Andy and Tommy). They both came from the same village. Which?

2   Give the Christian names of three McInallys who have played for Celtic.

3   One Celtic player's name began with Mac but, although he was Scottish, his name was not. Who am I talking about?

4   Christian name Adam, and generally regarded to be one of Celtic's best ever left-wingers. His absence from the Scottish Cup final of 1926 probably cost Celtic the Cup. Who was he?

5   In what year did John McPhail score the only goal of the Scottish Cup final?

6   John's brother Billy is famous for one particular feat. What?

7   Jimmy 'Napoleon' McMenemy won the Scottish Cup at Celtic Park. Yet Cup finals were played on a neutral venue. How is this possible?

8   One of Celtic's greatest ever full-backs was killed in the First World War. His nickname was 'Slasher'. Who was he?

9   Tom McAdam was a good centre half. On several occasions he played against his brother Colin. Who did Colin play for?

10 Everyone has heard of Jimmy McGrory. What was his middle name?

11 This Mc had the same name as a Dundee poet. He played at the same time as McGrory.

12 Which Mac earned the nickname 'Rhino' for his tenacious style of play?

Round

2

Bad Bhoys?

I'm hesitant to use the term 'bad'. Perhaps this round should be
named 'unfulfilled potential' or 'deviant aberrations'. It is about
men who have played for the club and who, for one reason or
another, have let themselves or the club down. Some, however,
are indeed bad in every sense of the word.

1 Before his career went downhill, George Connelly was
   a youngster of immense talent. How did he first show
   his talent?

2 Following a game on 4 February 1928, Tommy McInally
   disappeared. Who had Celtic just been playing?

3   Dick Beattie, Celtic's goalkeeper in the 1950s, was given nine months in jail for match-fixing in 1965. For which English team was he playing at the time?

4   Celtic lost a Cup tie in 1897 thanks in part to the non-appearance of Dan Doyle. Who were the opponents?

5   On at least two occasions Jimmy Johnstone was given a club suspension by Jock Stein. Why was he given one after a game against Queen's Park in 1967?

6   New Year's Day 1965 held no happy memories for Jimmy Johnstone. Why not?

7   Maurice Johnston will never be forgiven. Why not?

8   Why was Tommy Duff sacked in the aftermath of New Year's Day 1892?

9 Which Celtic player once, apparently, headbutted Henrik Larsson after an argument at training?

10 Which Celtic player and Scottish internationalist was found asphyxiated in a lime kiln in 1903 having been dismissed by the army as 'incorrigible and worthless'?

11 A member of the Lisbon Lions was once left out of a Cup final team on a Saturday for having been sent off while playing for Scotland in midweek, who?

12 Why did Johnny Browning, left-winger in Celtic's great 1914 team, find himself in jail in 1924?

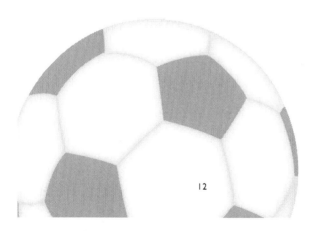

Round 3

Between the Wars

The years between 1918 and 1939 were crucial in world history in that the world, having survived one terrible war at awful cost, was unable to prevent the same thing happening again. There was also a sustained inability to improve everyone's standard of living, or rather to ensure a more equitable distribution of the world's resources. Celtic suffered from the economic depression more than most clubs, but it must also be said that the club's organisation did not help, as the despotism of Willie Maley, so successful before the First World War, did not always work in the best interests of the club in the 1920s and the 1930s. Yet there were great moments too.

1   How often did Celtic win the Scottish League in the 1920s and 1930s?

2   Celtic played a Scottish Cup final in the 1920s against a Second Division club. Who was this?

3   Which two players did Celtic transfer to Sunderland in 1928?

4   Maley, despicably, tried to sell Jimmy McGrory to Arsenal
    in 1928. McGrory, however, would not go. What was
    the reason given for Maley's desire to sell McGrory?

5   In the 1931 Cup final, Celtic had three Thomsons playing
    for them. What were their Christian names?

6   The opponents in the 1931 and 1933 Cup finals were
    Motherwell. What great thing happened to Motherwell
    in 1932?

7   Who was the ex-Celt who played for Motherwell at
    this time?

8   In 1936 Scotland beat Germany 2–0 at Ibrox in a result
    that (allegedly) put Hitler off his food for several days.
    Which Celtic player scored the two goals?

9   In 1937 Scotland and England drew a record crowd to
    Hampden; a week later a similar amount attended
    the Scottish Cup final between Celtic and Aberdeen.
    Who was the only player to play in both games?

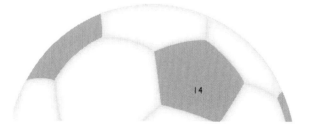

10 The Empire Exhibition Trophy was won on 10 June 1938 when Celtic beat Everton 1–0. Which two teams did Celtic beat on their way to the final?

11 Who scored Celtic's goal in the final of that tournament?

12 On the Saturday between Hitler's invasion of Poland on the Friday and the declaration of war on the Sunday, who did Celtic beat 1–0 at Parkhead?

Round

4

Disasters

By disasters, we do not mean disasters in the sense of the loss of life – these are perhaps tragedies – we are talking about footballing disasters. There have been a great deal of these, it must be admitted, but then again over the course of a century and a quarter, there are likely to be a few off days. Fortunately, we have managed to come back. Let's hope that we do not bring back too many unhappy memories!

1   On the evening of 15 May 1963, what happened?

2   In the dreadful European Cup final of 1970, who scored Celtic's goal?

3   Why did depression fill the air before the first game of the 1977/78 season, even though the team had last year won the League and Cup double?

4 When Celtic went out of the Scottish Cup, at the first time of asking, to Clyde in January 2006, which two players were making their Celtic debut?

5 On a Monday night in 1961/62, Celtic defeated a team 5–0, then lost to them 1–3 in the Scottish Cup semi-final the following Saturday. Which team?

6 Fortunately it was wartime and considered unofficial, but what was the score at Ibrox Park on New Year's Day 1943?

7 The disaster in the Scottish Cup against Inverness Caledonian Thistle in February 2000 was significant in the long-term history of the club, but it might not have happened if the game had been played on its originally scheduled date of 29 January. What was the reason for the postponement?

8 What happened to Celtic in Scotland's first ever domestic game to be televised live?

9 In which country did Celtic lose the World Club Championship in 1967?

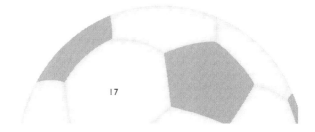

10 Celtic heartbreakingly lost the Scottish Cup final of
1990 on a penalty shoot-out. What was the final score
after 90 minutes?

11 When Celtic lost the Scottish Cup semi-final to
Ross County in 2010, the son of a famous ex-Celt was
playing for the Staggies. Who was the famous ex-Celt?

12 Celtic infamously lost the third game of the Glasgow Cup
final 0–4 in October 1908. This game was widely believed
to have been 'fixed'. Who were the winners?

Round

5

Europe

Celtic have participated in European competition since 1962, occasionally not being good enough to qualify for entry, but more often exiting miserably before Christmas. There have been high spots, yes, but more often than not, disappointment has been the order of the day. However, we would not live without it, especially since it does produce the money!

1 Who were Celtic's first ever European opponents on 26 September 1962?

2 En route to Lisbon in 1967, whom did Celtic beat at Parkhead with a late goal headed by Billy McNeill from a Charlie Gallagher corner kick?

3 Celtic have beaten three English teams in European competitions. Who are they?

4 The European Cup semi-final of 1972 went to a penalty shoot-out. All the penalties were successfully converted apart from one. Who was the unlucky player?

5 Celtic have had some good performances at the Nou Camp. In what year was their first appearance there?

6 When Celtic played Real Madrid in the European Cup quarter-final in 1980, they won the first leg 2–0. Who scored the goals?

7 At least two players have won European Cup medals after they left Parkhead. Who are the two well-known candidates?

8 And can you name one who arrived at Parkhead with one already in his possession?

9 In Celtic's march to the European Cup final of 1970, can you name the Italian team that they beat in the quarter-final?

10 In 2002/03, Celtic reached the final of the UEFA Cup, but who put them out of the European Champions' League?

11 In the Champion's League campaign of 2012/13, which ex-Celt played against them?

12 In 2013, Celtic lost to Juventus. They also lost to Juventus in 1981/82. Which Celtic manager played for Juventus at that time?

Round 6

Foreign Players

The time has now long gone when Celtic's team consisted of Scottish players, with perhaps the occasional Irishman or Englishman. Famously, the Lisbon Lions were entirely Scottish. Times have changed, and there have been the occasional days when Celtic have taken the field without a single Scotsman. Foreign players are a part of life. Whether this has made Celtic a better side or not, we leave the readers to make their own mind up.

1   Welsh people are hardly foreign, but can you name the three Welshmen who have played for Celtic in the twenty-first century?

2   What nationality was Stiliyan Petrov?

3   Who was the Canadian goalkeeper who played for Celtic in the 1930s?

4 A Danish goalkeeper played mainly for Dunfermline in the late 1960s, but he was briefly on Celtic's books. (His Christian name was a distinctly unfortunate one for a goalkeeper or indeed any football player to have!)

5 Who was Celtic's Icelandic central defender of the 1970s?

6 A Belgian defender played at Hampden on two successive weekends in 2001. Who?

7 In autumn 1965, four youngsters were given a prolonged trial at Celtic Park in what seemed like one of Jock Stein's successful propaganda stunts to keep Celtic on the back pages of the newspapers and relegate Rangers to obscurity. What nationality were these youngsters?

8 Which Frenchman joined Celtic in 2000 via Raith Rovers and Hibs?

9 Which member of the Celtic squad in 2012 was born in a town called Tegucigalpa?

10 Who is the only Celt to have won the African Cup of Nations?

11 Which three English teams did Mark Viduka play for after he left Celtic?

12 What nationality was Eyal Berkovic?

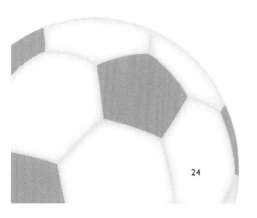

Round

7

Founding Fathers

It is easy to assume that Celtic have always been a big club. Not so. In the early days so much was against them, and Celtic owes so much to the tenacity and perseverance of their men of vision who made sure that the club could rise from very humble beginnings to be the huge worldwide institution that it is today. Much of these days are of course enshrined in legends rather than proven fact, but hopefully this round will reveal exactly how much you know of the origins of the club that means so much to us all.

1   Twenty years before the foundation of Celtic, Pat Welsh had met Willie Maley's father. In what circumstances?

2   When Willie Maley was invited to go along to Celtic Park for the first time, he wasn't the primary target. Who was?

3 Michael Davitt famously planted shamrocks on the turf of the new Celtic Park in March 1892. What disability did Davitt suffer from?

4 Also in 1892 Celtic won three cups. According to legend, what did Ned McGinn suggest that they should do in the Vatican to celebrate?

5 What was the name of the man who came from Renton to be centre half and captain of the new Celtic club?

6 The first ever game at Old Celtic Park did not feature Celtic. Who were the teams who played there on 8 May 1888?

7 Celtic's first game was against Rangers. Their second game was against a Dundee team recruited to a large extent from the Dundee Irish community in Lochee. What was this team called?

8 Who scored Celtic's first ever goal?

9 Which founding father of Celtic was instrumental in the founding of the Scottish League in 1890?

10 Technically, when Celtic were founded, the game was all amateur. In what year was professionalism legalised in Scotland?

11 Which Celt who played in the first ever game became the first coach of Slavia Prague?

12 Which early Celt was known as 'the Duke'?

Round

8

Henrik Larsson

Few players have brought such excitement and adoration to the Celtic crowd as Henrik Larsson. His ability to turn at speed, to score all kinds of goals – both the spectacular and the mundane tap-ins – and his sheer professionalism and commitment to the club guaranteed that he would become one of Parkhead's all-time greats, and that he would be freely compared to Jimmy Quinn and Jimmy McGrory.

1 From whom was he signed in 1997?

2 Against whom did he make his competitive debut?

3 What was the first medal that he won for Celtic?

4 What misfortune befell him on 22 October 1999?

5 In season 2000/01 how many goals did he score in all competitions for Celtic?

6 He scored a hat-trick in the Scottish League Cup final of
   March 2001. Who were the opposition?

7 What influence does Magdalena Spjuth have on him?

8 Who were the opposition when he broke his jaw on
   9 February 2003?

9 His last competitive game for Celtic was the Scottish Cup
   final of 2004 against Dunfermline Athletic. He scored
   twice in the 3–1 win. Who scored the other goal?

10 He won a European Cup winner's medal with Barcelona.
   Who did they beat in the final?

11 How many times did he play for Sweden?

12 He played briefly for one other British club. Which was it?

Round

9

Irish Players

In spite of the well-documented fact that Celtic were founded by the Irish in Glasgow, comparatively few native Irishmen have played for Celtic over the past 125 years. There have been some very influential ones however.

1   Who ended a long and successful career with a big English club and finished off his career with a Scottish League Cup medal for Celtic?

2   Who was called 'The Mighty Atom' and is generally regarded as one of the best players of all time?

3   When Pat Bonner was injured before the 1988 Scottish Cup final, he was replaced by another Irishman. Who?

4 Chris Morris played for the Republic of Ireland, but wasn't born in Ireland. Where was he born?

5 Celtic have had four managers born in Ireland. Who are they?

6 I was born in Belfast in 1924, and my middle name is Patrick. Who am I?

7 Which Irish full-back played in the same team as John Thomson in 1931?

8 I have the same surname as a bird. Who am I?

9 This fellow was actually born in Scotland, but played for the Republic of Ireland in 1967.

10 What position did Sean Fallon play in the 1954
Scottish Cup final?

11 What was significant about Pat Bonner's signing for
Celtic in 1978?

12 Joe Haverty played one game for Celtic in 1964.
For what English teams did he play?

Round 10

Jimmy McGrory

The name James 'Jimmy' McGrory is irreversibly associated with Celtic, and will stay so for evermore. There will be very few left who saw McGrory play, but everyone has heard of him and will recall at third or fourth hand what he did – his famous goals, his chivalrous behaviour to opponents, and his total commitment to the club that he loved. His managerial career was a disappointment, but he did nevertheless have his moments, and when Jock Stein took over in 1965, Jock insisted that his players call McGrory 'Boss'. His death in 1982 was a cause of sadness to Celtic supporters everywhere.

1 With which club did McGrory win the Scottish Junior Cup in 1922? (Typically he headed one of the goals in their 2–1 victory!)

2 He was farmed out to another club in the 1923/24 season. Which?

3 He headed home the winning goal in the epic Scottish Cup final of 1925 against Dundee. It was from a free kick. Who took the free kick?

4 He was injured and unable to play in the 1927 Scottish Cup final. Who took his place at centre forward?

5 In the 1933 Scotland *v.* England international, he is credited for having created the Hampden Roar. Which Rangers player passed to him to score?

6 Two weeks after that game, he scored the only goal of the game in the Scottish Cup final. Who were the opponents?

7 What was significant about his hat-trick in the 5–3 win against Aberdeen at Parkhead on midwinter's day 1935?

8 On 14 March 1936 he scored a hat-trick against Motherwell. How long did it take him?

9 How many League goals did he score in season 1935/36?

10 Which team did he become manager of in 1937?

11 In what year was he appointed manager of Celtic?

12 As manager of Celtic, he managed one League and Cup double. In what year?

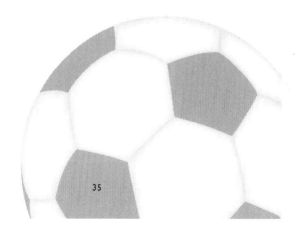

Jimmy Quinn

Now over 100 years have passed since the floruit of Jimmy Quinn, but everyone through the century knew and talked about the feats of this great man. In his time he was a personality and everyone in the British Isles knew who he was, but, paradoxically, he was a socially inept man who hated publicity, was painfully shy and lived for nothing other than coal mining, his family, football and his beloved team. Even when not playing for them, he went with the team, on one occasion being seen carrying the hamper off a train, smoking a clay pipe and 'looking just like an ordinary man'. If you score poorly in this round, and do not know enough about Jimmy, then may we suggest that you read a little more about him. It will enrich your knowledge of Celtic!

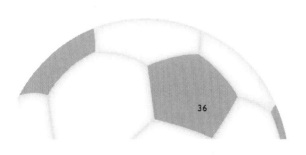

1 From which Dunbartonshire mining village did Quinn come?

2 What was the name of the junior team he played for?

3 He is better known as a centre forward, but what was his first position?

4 In what competition in 1902 did he score a hat-trick against Rangers at Cathkin Park?

5 In the Scottish Cup final of 1904, Quinn scored another hat-trick against Rangers. What was particularly significant about the venue of this game?

6 Quinn was sent off in the Scottish Cup semi-final of 1905. What was the name of the Rangers player whom he was wrongly accused of deliberately kicking?

7 Many of his goals were scored by 'charging'.
What exactly does this mean?

8 In which city did Jimmy Quinn score four goals for
Scotland in 1908?

9 How many times did he play for Scotland in total?

10 How many Scottish Cup winners' medals did he win?

11 In what year did he play his last game for Celtic?

12 What personal tragedy did he suffer in 1944?

Jock Stein

Jock Stein dominated Scottish football in his days as Celtic manager. He was one of the few characters immediately recognised by everyone, even those who did not like or understand football. He was used by the BBC as 'Mr Scotland' in their TV programmes, and was well known in Europe as well. He had his unpleasant side, no doubt, as some of his ex-players would testify, but he was a big man in every sense of the word. On one occasion, when a Kilmarnock player was badly injured on a cold day, he took off his overcoat and threw it over the injured man as he lay on the stretcher. On another occasion, a few weeks after Lisbon in 1967, he sent a football, signed by all the players, to a very sick boy in a Kirkcaldy hospital. But then again, great men do great things!

1   In what year was Jock Stein born?

2   For which Welsh club did he play before signing for Celtic?

3 Which special one-off trophy did Stein captain Celtic to victory in 1953?

4 In the team that won the Scottish Cup in 1954 against Aberdeen, Jock was the centre half. Who were the right half and the left half?

5 Why was 26 April 1961 a happy night for Jock Stein, but not for Celtic?

6 Which Scottish club was Stein the manager of immediately before he became manager of Celtic in 1965?

7 How many times did Celtic win the Scottish League Championship under Jock Stein?

8   Apart from the famous year of 1967, there was another
    year in which Celtic won all three Scottish domestic
    trophies in the calendar month of April. Which year are
    we talking about?

9   Name the two centre forwards whom Jock Stein signed
    from Motherwell.

10 Complete the following much quoted statement of
    Jock Stein: 'Football without the ... is nothing'.

11 Which English club did he manage briefly before
    becoming manager of Scotland?

12 He died in particularly tragic circumstances, but in a way
    which was fitting for him. When and where?

Round
13

Lisbon 1967

The European Cup triumph of 1967 was the most famous game that Celtic have ever played in, and one which will remain enshrined in Celtic folklore for evermore with the names of Simpson, Craig and Gemmell; Murdoch, McNeill and Clark; Johnstone, Wallace, Chalmers, Lennox and Auld. (Some say Auld and Lennox – but let's not argue!) For those of us lucky enough to be alive on that day, it was indeed the best day of our lives, as the words of a song put it. And how we wish that we could repeat it! Young Celtic fans deserve a similar day to remember!

1   On what day of the week was 25 May 1967?

2   Who was Celtic's substitute goalkeeper?

3   For what purpose did Jock Stein use his reserve players immediately before the game?

4   What did Bertie Auld do in the tunnel before the game?

5   Which member of the Lisbon team already had a European losers' medal?

6   Prior to 1967, how often had Inter Milan won the European Cup?

7   What was the name of the English BBC commentator who said unashamedly that he was supporting Celtic?

8   Stevie Chalmers scored the winning goal, but who sent in the ball?

9   Which Celtic defender had the bad luck to concede a dubious penalty?

10   Which Inter Milan player was injured and unable to play?

11   Less than a fortnight after this game, Celtic had another famous victory. Whom did they beat?

12   Sadly, it did not last long. Which team put Celtic out of the following year's European Cup in October 1967?

Long, Long Ago

The cut-off point for this one is the outbreak of the
First World War in 1914, so we are really looking for the
antiquarians here. Yet this era was probably Celtic's most
successful, and deserves to be recalled, even though those
who saw Jimmy Quinn and Jimmy McMenemy have now
sadly long passed on. But when I die, I, for one, am looking
forward to the possibility (depending on one's religious
views, of course) of going to the other paradise and meeting
the great men of Celtic's early history. What a day that will
be for the Celtic geeks like myself and all of you who score
well in this round!

1   Who were the opponents when Celtic won the
    Scottish Cup for the first time in 1892?

2   Which tournament did Celtic win five years in a row
    between 1892 and 1896?

3   What happened on 28 November 1896?

4 Which team did Celtic beat 11–0 on 26 October 1895?

5 At least two members of the nineteenth-century Celtic team had the Christian name Dan. Name the two most well known.

6 Which Englishman won a Scottish Cup medal in 1899 to add to the English Cup medal that he had won for Aston Villa in 1895?

7 The 1902 Scottish Cup final between Celtic and Hibs was played at Celtic Park. Why was this?

8 What innovation took place on 15 August 1903?

9 Why was Celtic's game on 2 February 1901 postponed?

10 Which future manager of Aberdeen and Clyde played unsuccessfully as an inside forward for Celtic in season 1911/12?

11 What was the name of the player who played for
Celtic between 1907 and 1909, then went on to
have a long and varied career with other clubs and
eventually scored more goals than Jimmy McGrory?
He also scored the goal for Dundee in the 1925
Scottish Cup final.

12 With war only a few months away in 1914, Celtic, whilst
on a tour in Budapest, played against the English Cup
winners in a 1–1 draw. Which team was this?

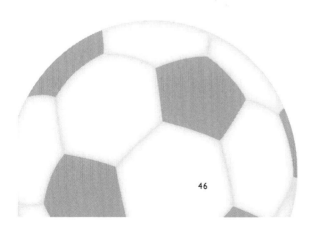

Round 15

Managers

Celtic have had two great managers in Maley and Stein, and several other good ones including McNeill, O'Neill and Strachan. Others like McGrory and Hay had their moments but some, one fears, will not go down in history as having been great leaders of the club. The jury is still out on Neil Lennon of course, but it is likely that he will join the good and possibly even the great ones. Time will tell.

1   Jimmy McStay was manager of Celtic in unfortunate times during the Second World War. He was also manager of two other Scottish clubs. Name them.

2   How often did Jimmy McGrory win the Scottish League as manager of Celtic?

3   Jimmy McGrory's last game as manager was a Scottish Cup quarter-final match at Parkhead in 1965. Who were the opponents?

4 Before Wim Jansen became manager in 1997, Celtic had already met him in unfortunate circumstances. When?

5 Following Liam Brady's sacking in 1993 and the appointment of Lou Macari, who was Celtic's interim manager who never lost a game?

6 Davie Hay won the Scottish Cup once as manager of Celtic. Who scored the winning goal in the final?

7 Billy McNeill won the Scottish League Cup only once as manager of Celtic. Which team did Celtic beat in the final?

8 The catalyst for the sacking of the unfortunate Tony Mowbray was a 0–4 thrashing. Who beat Celtic that night?

9 Which English team did Jo Venglos manage?

10 Who was Celtic's manager when they won the Scottish League Cup in 2000?

11 Which Scottish team, other than Aberdeen, did Gordon Strachan play for?

12 Which Scottish team, other than Celtic, did Jock Stein play for?

Round 16

Nicknames

Nicknames are of course a part of football culture, and such is Glasgow humour that quite a few Celtic players have picked up nicknames, some complimentary, some otherwise. Most teams have nicknames as well.

1 He was called 'Shuggy' or 'Chuggy' for reasons that are unrepeatable, but nevertheless widely known. Who was he?

2 'The Artful Dodger' jumped ship to go to Rangers, but played a great deal better for Celtic than he did for Rangers. He later managed Third Lanark.

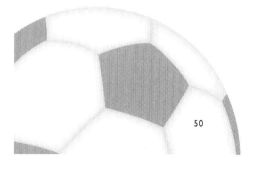

3 The faither of 'Faither' played for Rangers.
Who was 'Faither'?

4 Twice in the early 1990s, Celtic played the 'Loons' in
the Scottish Cup. Who are the 'Loons'?

5 Some of his players called their manager 'Sweeties'
(but not to his face!) because of his habit of
eating sweets. Who was he?

6 What was the nickname of Jimmy McMenemy?

7 Which player of the 1930s was given the nickname
'Happy Feet'?

8 Everyone knows that John Hughes of the 1960s had the
nickname 'Yogi Bear', and the other John Hughes of
the 1990s inherited it. But which Dundee player of
the 1960s (and often a direct opponent of the first
John Hughes) had the same nickname?

9 Why was Billy McNeill called 'Caesar'?

10 Which player, who played the role of sweeper, earned the nickname 'The Brush'?

11 James Young played for Celtic from 1903 until 1916. By what nickname was he almost universally known?

12 On a trip to Europe, this player earned the nickname from a foreign journalist of the 'Flying Flea'. Who are we talking about?

Round

17

Opponents

Before you can play football, you must have someone to play against. A wise manager will realise that in a run-up to a game, the most important team in the world is the one we are playing against, and that you really have to assume they are as good as Barcelona or Real Madrid.

1 In Celtic's great 1966/67 season, one team beat them both home and away. Who was that?

2 On 30 December 1922, it was Celtic's pleasure to hansel in a new stand. Celtic won 3–0, the stand is still in existence and Celtic played in front of it in 2013. Which ground are we talking about?

3 Of the forty-two teams in the Scottish Leagues, there is one team that Celtic have never played a competitive fixture against. Who is this?

4 Who was the first team ever to beat Celtic?

5 Which team that is no longer in existence has beaten Celtic in a Scottish Cup final?

6 Celtic have won the Scottish Cup most times, Rangers are next, but who are third?

7 Celtic played several times at Marine Gardens. Who were the hosts?

8 Which team, in the opinion of Bobby Murdoch, (apart from Rangers) gave Celtic the hardest games in the glory years from 1965 to 1975?

9 On 28 January 1996 Celtic played at Easter Road, but not against Hibs. Who were their opponents?

10 On 27 April 1968, Jock Stein took his team to see the
    Scottish Cup final. Who were the participants?

11 And on that very day, what particular piece of good
    news did Celtic receive?

12 There are four teams from Fife in the Scottish League,
    but Celtic have played another two in the Scottish Cup.
    Who are they?

Patsy Gallacher

There was a surprising unanimity among those who saw him that Patsy Gallacher was the greatest of them all. His trickery, his passing ability and his love of the game meant he was much admired by friends and opponents alike. The fact that his career was on both sides of a terrible war in some ways intensified the feelings that were expressed about him. He was indeed 'the most talked about man in the trenches' and my late father would always conclude any discussion about football and footballers by saying 'Look, I saw Patsy Gallacher!' And that was the end of that!

I He was born in Milford Poor House and lived most of his early life in Ramelton. In which county in Ireland is that?

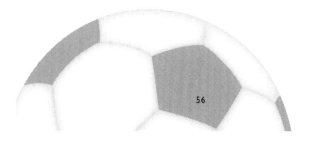

2 In what year did he make his debut for Celtic?

3 How many Scottish Cup medals did he win?

4 He played mainly as an inside right. What change did this necessitate in team selection in 1912?

5 Why did he have to serve a lengthy suspension in season 1916/17?

6 Why did he use the away dressing room at Celtic Park on 13 March 1920?

7 Everyone knows that he scored that wonder goal in the Scottish Cup final against Dundee in 1925, but he also masterminded the team to a 5–0 victory in the semi-final. Against whom?

8 What was his job outside football after the war?

9 For which team did he play after Celtic?

10   What song did the Celtic supporters sing in his honour
     at Ibrox in the Scottish Cup semi-final of 1927?

11   His nephew played for Celtic in the Empire Exhibition
     Trophy of 1937. Who was this?

12   For what team did his son Tommy play in the early 1950s?

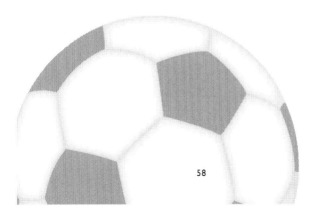

Round 19

Pictures

There is nothing more fascinating than old pictures. One curses inventors for being so slow to discover modern technology so that we could watch games in action, in colour and with repeated playbacks! Unfortunately we have to make do with what we have. Here are some interesting pictures, which will test your knowledge.

1 This is the Celtic team of 1907/08. What are the three trophies in the picture?

2 It's tricky to spot the goalkeeper in this picture. This is because goalkeepers did not wear different jerseys until a few years later. The goalkeeper was David Adams. Which is he?

3 This team absolutely hotched with brilliant players. Can you identify Sunny Jim Young?

4 Jimmy 'Napoleon' McMenemy was a tricky wee player. The word 'wee' might be a clue to his identification.

5 And no Celtic team was ever complete without the mighty Quinn. Where is Jimmy?

6 Celtic have just won the Scottish Cup in 1954.
Who are the two Celtic players in the photograph?

7 Which team did they beat in the final?

8 Who is the Celtic player whom Billy McNeill has in a headlock in this picture?

9 What is the occasion?

10 Celtic have played many great games on this ground.
This is an early picture of it. Whose ground is it?

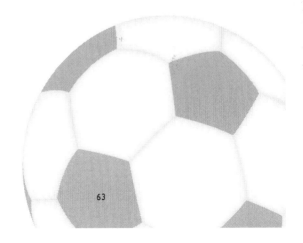

11 What event is depicted here?

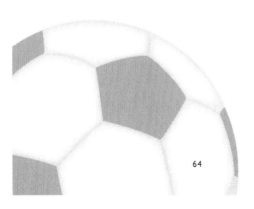

12 Which great Celtic player is shown in this picture
    against Partick Thistle at Firhill?

Round

20

Quotes

No responsibility can be taken for the verbatim accuracy of the following quotes, but they were all said or attributed to people with Celtic connections. Sometimes the immediate context has to be given in the form of what was said before.

1 'The Celtic jersey does not shrink to fit inferior players.'

2 'My life without Celtic would have been a very empty one indeed.'

3 'So scoring a hat-trick in a Hampden final puts you in the same bracket as Jimmy Quinn.' 'Aye, but I did it twice!'

4 'I'll no need tae go!'

5 'It's not a man's creed or nationality that counts, it's the man himself.'

6   'I cannot claim like other Celts that Celtic were my
    first love, but I know that they will be my greatest
    and the longest lasting.'

7   'Face the ball, Celts!'

8   'Not one thin dime will they get from me!'

9   'This is not the end, just the beginning.'

10 '… good enough for the homeless …'

11 'John, you're immortal now!'

12 (After rolling back the bedclothes) 'At least, Willie,
    these legs have done their bit for the Celtic.'

Round

21

Records

The historian soon learns that he must be very careful about records. Attendances are often vague in the old days, and goalscorers must be treated with suspicion because the only real source is newspapers, and they quite often disagree! Nor will any club, neither the buying nor the selling one, be necessarily willing to divulge transfer fees, and often the press have to make up a figure. Nevertheless, even allowing for these qualifications, Celtic have a very impressive collection of records.

I   Billy McNeill has the top number of appearances in all competitions for the club, but who has the record League appearances?

2   Everyone probably knows that Jimmy McGrory is Celtic's most prolific goalscorer, but who is second?

3 Jimmy McGrory set a Scottish record by scoring 8 goals in a game in January 1928. Who were the luckless opponents?

4 The record attendance in the European Cup involved Celtic. Who were they playing?

5 The record attendance for a Scottish Cup final was set in 1937. Who were Celtic's opponents that day?

6 Also in 1937 (the Friday night after that Scottish Cup final) came Celtic's record defeat. Who defeated them 8–0?

7 Who is Celtic's most capped player?

8 What Scottish Premier League record did Celtic create on the occasion of their 123rd birthday (6 November 2010)?

9 What record did Celtic set between 13 November 1915 and 21 April 1917?

10　When were Celtic first involved in a penalty shoot-out in a competitive game?

11　The record attendance for a game at Celtic Park is given as 92,000. (The figure being exactly 92,000 immediately makes one suspicious.) It was set on a New Year's Day game against Rangers. In what year?

12　At what ground did Celtic set a ground record attendance and win the Scottish League on the same day in 1922?

Round 22

Scottish Cup

In many ways, this is Celtic's favourite trophy which they have won more often than anyone else. It is the oldest trophy in the world (first played for in 1874) and is now so old that it remains in the Hampden Park Museum apart from when it is presented to the winning captain at the end of the final. It is then put back in its case, and the winners are issued with a replica trophy. It has been called the 'blue riband' and was considered in the old days to be of more importance than the Scottish League.

1 On how many occasions have Celtic won the Scottish Cup at Ibrox?

2 Who scored the two goals for Celtic that won the Scottish Cup in 1967?

3 How often have Celtic beaten Rangers in the final of the Scottish Cup?

4 Which team defeated Celtic at the semi-final stage twice in the space of four years between 1959 and 1962?

5 Who missed a penalty kick in the Scottish Cup final of 2005?

6 Who scored a goal in every round bar one in the 1923 Scottish Cup?

7 In what year was there a Hampden riot which started after the Cup had been presented to Celtic?

8 A previous Hampden riot was sparked off by the perception that both teams were 'at it'. When was this? (It was believed that they had deliberately drawn in 2 games and were now wanting a third big game, and therefore there would be no extra time at the end of the second game.)

9 Celtic's worst ever Scottish Cup final was possibly 1963 when they went down 0–3 to Rangers in a replay. Yet they had played well enough in the first game, which was a 1–1 draw. Who scored Celtic's goal?

10 In what two years have Inverness Caledonian Thistle dismissed Celtic from the Scottish Cup?

11 Jimmy Quinn famously scored a hat-trick in the 1904 Scottish Cup final. He had a less happy experience the following year in the semi-final. Why?

12 Which team, no longer in existence, did Celtic beat in the semi-final of the 1990 Scottish Cup?

Scottish League Cup

The Scottish League Cup is often described as the Cinderella Trophy or the 'Diddy Cup'. It started during the Second World War as the Southern League Cup and became the Scottish League Cup in season 1946/47. It is grossly unfair to dismiss it as some tournament of secondary importance, but it is true that Celtic lag way behind Rangers in this competition. Yet, there have also been some fine performances, and we should be proud of our record here as well.

1   Everyone knows that Celtic beat Rangers 7–1 on 19 October 1957, but who scored Rangers' only goal?

2   Who did Celtic beat in their first League Cup final?

3 At the time of that game, which club held the record for League Cup victories?

4 Who are the four Celtic players who have scored hat-tricks in Scottish League Cup finals?

5 Celtic won the Scottish League Cup for five years in a row from 1965/66 until 1969/70. All finals were played in the month of October apart from the one in 1968/69 which was played in April. Why was that?

6 Celtic reached the Scottish League Cup final for a record fourteen times in a row between 1964 and 1978. During that time, they lost finals to four teams (not including Rangers). Who were they?

7 Celtic beat Kilmarnock 3–0 in the Scottish League Cup final of 2001. Which Celtic player was sent off that day?

8 In the Scottish League Cup final of 2006, a player scored the last goal in the 3—0 victory to win him his only medal of a long and distinguished career. Who?

9 Who scored 2 penalties in the first half of a Scottish League Cup final against Rangers?

10 Jo Venglos had a managerial career of one Scottish League Cup game. Who were the opponents?

11 All Celtic's Scottish League Cup victories were at Hampden, apart from one which was at Ibrox. Who were the opponents in that final?

12 Celtic have played Scottish League Cup finals against all the teams in this list apart from one. Which is the odd one out? Hibs, Aberdeen, Raith Rovers, Hearts, St Johnstone or Dunfermline Athletic?

Round

24

Scottish League

Since 1890, the Scottish League (in whatever form, SPL, SPFL or simply Scottish League) has been the bread and butter of Scottish football. Sadly Celtic's total number of championships lags behind that of Rangers, and this is perhaps explained by the perception that, over the decades, Celtic have been adventurous, exciting and spectacular but infuriatingly inconsistent, whereas Rangers (certainly in the Willie Struth era) have been more mechanical but also more reliable.

1   In what year did Celtic win the Scottish League for the first time?

2   Celtic won the Scottish League six years in a row from 1905 until 1910. What were the rather unusual circumstances of the winning of the first of these championships?

3 On what ground did Celtic in April 1972 break their own record of winning six championships in a row?

4 On at least two occasions in the twenty-first century, Celtic have lost the League on the final day of the season. One of these was the day at Motherwell known as Black Sunday. Which future Celtic player scored for Motherwell that day in May 2005?

5 Which team were Rangers playing that day in 2005?

6 Against which team did Celtic confirm the League Championship in their centenary year of 1988?

7 What role did Albert Kidd play in winning the championship in 1986?

8 In Celtic's League-winning season of 1935/36, who was the goalkeeper?

9 Celtic were once almost relegated from the Scottish First Division in 1948. On what ground did they grab a famous victory to preserve their status?

10 When Celtic won the League in 1908, it was actually won on 25 April (against Rangers at Ibrox), which was manager Willie Maley's birthday. How old was he?

11 Famously in 1909, Celtic won 8 games in twelve days to win the Scottish League. Which team ended up second that year?

12 In the 1890s, Celtic won the Scottish League four years out of six between 1893 and 1898. Which team won the League in both 1895 and 1897?

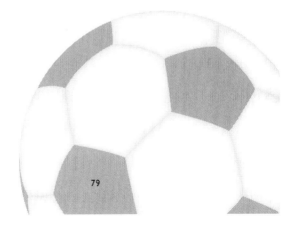

25

Songs and Singers

Celtic have always had many songs. Some of them are
unprintable, but many are funny, inspiring and tuneful.
There have also been many people with Celtic connections
who have been singers.

1 In what year was 'The Celtic Song' released?

2 In the 1930s Celtic supporters adapted the words of
   a redemptionist hymn 'Tell me the old, old story'.
   The next line was 'a hat-trick for …' Who?

3 Which Celtic goalkeeper released a disc of
   'The Dear Little Shamrock'?

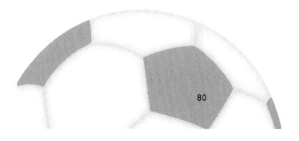

4 In 1964 the song 'Celtic! Celtic!' was released, and one of the lines detailing the current team's forwards ran 'Jim Johnstone, Murdoch, Chalmers, _____ and John Hughes'. Who is the missing inside left?

5 Round about the same time, Callum Kennedy released a Celtic song as well. In it he claimed that supporters came to watch Celtic from two rural Scottish towns. One was Crieff. What was the other one?

6 In 1931, soon after the tragic death of John Thomson, a song was produced which ran 'A Young Lad named John Thomson ...' and then it mentioned the name of the Fife junior team that John played for. What was John's junior football team?

7 A song used to be sung which began 'Said Lizzie to Phillip as they sat to dine ...' What Celtic triumph did this commemorate?

8 Which famous Celtic supporter and singer was born on 10 January 1945?

9 Why did Celtic supporters sing 'The Red Flag' at the Glasgow Charity Cup final of 1926?

10 In about 1969, Celtic supporters sang a song 'Aye, aye, aye, aye, we are the Glasgow Celtic!' In that song they claimed that Ronnie Simpson was better than whom?

11 Rangers supporters sing a song called 'No Surrender'. Following Celtic's 6–2 victory over Rangers in August 2000, what did Celtic fans claim that the cry was?

12 In a parody of an evangelical Christian song, what did Celtic supporters claim that Henrik Larsson was?

Round

26

Strange But True

Inevitably in the history of a football team, some strange things happen. Celtic are no exception. We cannot guarantee the absolute accuracy of some of these events since some are inevitably exaggerated, but we hope they won't be too far from the truth.

1   Which Celtic football player won two medals for the club before he even played a game at Celtic Park?

2   A Celtic player once forgot his boots before the first game of the season. He went home for them, got stuck in traffic and was late in arriving at Celtic Park. He was still in loads of time for the kick-off but was dropped from the team. Who was this?

3   Which Celtic player had an international career which lasted 18 minutes before he was badly injured?

4 Which Celtic player scored a goal for Scotland in his only international match? It was a header, and he scored it before he had even kicked a ball!

5 Jimmy Delaney won three Cup medals in three different countries in three different decades (with the Second World War in the middle!). He won the Scottish Cup with Celtic in 1937 the English Cup with Manchester United in 1948, but for which Irish team did he win the Irish Cup in 1954?

6 In 1959 Celtic beat Hearts 2–1. What unfortunate side effect did this victory have?

7 Bobby Lennox was wrongly ordered off in the World Club Championship of 1967. What persuaded him to leave the field instead of arguing with the referee?

8 At Bayview, Methil in 1973 what remarkable series of events occurred in a 2–2 draw between East Fife and Celtic?

9 Andy Lynch famously scored the penalty kick which won the Scottish Cup in 1977. What less happy experience did he have against Motherwell a few weeks earlier?

10 In the replay of the 1911 Scottish Cup final between Celtic and Hamilton Academical, what delayed the start of play?

11 Why was Johnny Doyle sent off in a game against Ayr United in August 1977?

12 What happened at half-time in the game between Partick Thistle *v.* Celtic at Firhill on 24 April 1982?

Round

27

The Dear Old Paradise

Celtic Park has a special meaning for most of us. Sometimes loosely called Parkhead, which is the area of the east end of Glasgow in which it is situated, the ground has in many ways reflected the times in which it finds itself. In the 1930s it was surrounded by heavy industry, in the 1950s, 1960s and 1970s it was housing, whereas nowadays, in the more affluent twenty-first century, it has a lovely view of the new Sir Chris Hoy Velodrome. Going to Celtic Park on a match day is comforting and reassuring. It is like going home.

1 In what year did Celtic move to the present Celtic Park?

2 Why was 1904 the last year in which Celtic Park was regularly used for the 'big' International between Scotland and England?

3 What nickname was given by supporters to the ugly barn structure on the north side of the ground?

4 In which year was the structure replaced?

5 Where the main stand is now, stood what is known as the Grant Stand. The club had a progressive idea of adding a glass front to keep out the wind and rain. Why did this idea have to be abandoned?

6 In the 1920s, a group of people were allowed to stand in front of the Grant Stand for free. Who were they?

7 Which profession was traditionally allowed in without payment to Celtic Park?

8 In what year were floodlights installed at Celtic Park?

9 Which end of the ground, 'west' or 'east', was looked upon as the traditional 'Celtic' end at Old Firm games?

10 When Celtic won the Scottish League for nine years in a row between 1966 and 1974, how many championships were secured at Celtic Park?

11 In the 1990s, two Scottish Cup finals was held at Celtic Park. Which years?

12 In a game against Raith Rovers in the Scottish League Cup in August 1995, what unusual problem affected the pitch?

Round 28

Wartime

Let us hope that there will never be another war. There were two horrible conflicts in the twentieth century as well as a host of smaller ones. The two major wars inevitably disrupted football, but it is a fallacy to think that wartime football was not taken seriously. On the contrary, football, like cinema, theatre and the arts, was looked upon as even more important for morale reasons, and results were eagerly anticipated and looked forward to in trenches, on the high seas, the desert, Italy and Burma. As far as Celtic was concerned, the First World War saw fine performances and much success; the Second World War was absolutely dreadful.

1 Who were Celtic's main challengers for the Scottish League in the 1914/15 season?

2 Because of wartime regulations which prohibited midweek play, what were Celtic compelled to do on 15 April 1916?

3 Who was the Fife-born half-back who lost his life at the Battle of Arras in 1917?

4 On 8 May 1915, Celtic beat Rangers 3–2 in the Glasgow Charity Cup final. What world-shattering event had taken place the day before?

5 Who was the centre forward who became known as 'the sniper' during the First World War?

6 Which Celtic captain won the Military Cross in October 1943?

7 Why was Jimmy Delaney unavailable to play for Celtic for the first two seasons of the Second World War?

8 George Gillan is not one of Celtic's better-known players. He did have his moment of glory, however, on 28 September 1940. What was it?

9 Which Scotsman, who later became a legendary manager with an English club, wanted to play for Celtic (whom he loved) during the Second World War, but Celtic never took the hint?

10 Celtic won the Glasgow Charity Cup in May 1943. Whom did they beat 3–0 in the final at Hampden?

11 Towards the end of the Second World War, a goalkeeper emerged who would become recognised as one of Celtic's best ever. Who was this?

12 On the day after VE Day, in 1945, Celtic won the Victory in Europe Cup by beating Queen's Park. There was something slightly unconventional in the way that they won it. What was it?

Round

29

Who Am I?

This round gives information about well-known characters in Celtic's history. The clues given are not always the most obvious ones and you have to guess who is speaking.

1   I was signed by Billy McNeill from Kilmarnock in 1978, and I am now a TV pundit and commentator. I suffered several years of illness.

2   I played in the Scottish Cup final of 1931, but took ill six months later and died of tuberculosis in December 1933.

3   Hardly anyone had heard of me when I joined the club, but soon after my arrival I inspired the club to a 5–1 win over Rangers in November 1998.

4 They called me the 'Wee Barra' because of my diminutive stature. Many people think that Celtic lost the 1955 Scottish Cup final replay because they dropped me. A full ten years later, I was still good enough to earn a Scottish cap!

5 I was born in Rutherglen, and earned the nickname of a famous French general. A week after the end of the First World War, I almost died of the 'flu' but I recovered and won another Scottish cap in 1920, when I was reckoned to be the oldest internationalist at the time.

6 I was also born in Rutherglen and played for Celtic in the 1960s. I was a competent inside forward, but it was only when the new manager changed my position that my career really took off. I also played for Middlesbrough.

7 I came from the Highlands and was Celtic's successor to Billy McNeill as centre half. I later played for Hearts.

8 They called me the 'Maestro', but it was my misfortune to play for the club in unsuccessful times. My brother played as well.

9 I learned a lot from Brian Clough but was no great success as a manager at two English clubs after I left Celtic Park.

10   I am probably the only man to have played for three Glasgow clubs as I played for Partick Thistle as well.

11   I could never understand the hatred that I incurred when I left Celtic Park because I was there for three seasons during which time we won the Scottish League twice and the Scottish League Cup once. I also won a Scottish Cup medal – but with another club against Celtic.

12   I grew up supporting Partick Thistle and had two spells at Celtic Park – my second being considerably better than my first. I have also appeared for Birmingham City and Hibs.

Round

30

Willie Maley

We've kept the star for last! Willie Maley is rightly looked upon as 'the man who made Celtic'. He played in the first game, was manager from 1897 until 1940, and unearthed many fine players for the club. His side of 1907 and 1908 has being regarded as the best in the world and, in terms of Celtic history, as good as Jock Stein's 1967 side. But he remains an enigmatic, mysterious and not always loveable character.

1 What was his father's profession?

2 What was the name of his wife?

3 What was his normal position in the team when he played?

4 Why did he sometimes call himself Willie Montgomery?

5 He was appointed manager/secretary in 1897 in the aftermath of a terrible Scottish Cup defeat at the hands of which non-League side?

6 How often did he play a full International for Scotland?

7 Which two sports, other than football, did he participate in?

8 Of whom did he say 'I always had a soft spot for the boy' even though he transferred him twice?

9 How many times did he win the Scottish Cup as a manager?

10 What was the name of his friend who was manager of Rangers and was drowned in a boating accident in the Clyde in 1920?

11 Which former player of his was he instrumental in bringing back to Celtic to be trainer and more or less assistant manager in the late 1930s?

12 In what year did he die?

THE ANSWERS

All the Macs

1 Croy.
2 There are five. Take your pick from Tommy, Alan, Jim, Arthur or John.
3 Lou Macari.
4 McLean.
5 1951.
6 He scored a hat-trick for Celtic in the 7–1 Scottish League Cup win over Rangers in 1957.
7 He was playing for Partick Thistle when they beat Rangers 1–0 in the Scottish Cup final of 1921 played at Celtic Park.
8 Donnie McLeod.
9 Rangers.
10 Edward.
11 William 'Peter' McGonagle.
12 Murdo MacLeod.

Bad Bhoys

1 By giving a demonstration of keepy-uppy at half-time in a European Cup Winners' Cup tie against Dynamo Kiev.
2 Keith.
3 Portsmouth.
4 Arthurlie.
5 For a violent indiscretion on an opponent, unnoticed by the referee.
6 He was sent off by referee Tom Wharton following a 'clash' with Theorelf Beck of Rangers.
7 He signed for Rangers in summer 1989, having said he would join Celtic.
8 For being drunk in Celtic's 0–8 defeat by Dumbarton.
9 Tosh McKinlay.
10 Mick McKeown.
11 Tommy Gemmell.
12 Match-fixing.

Between the Wars

Round 3

1   Four times.
2   East Fife.
3   Tommy McInally and Adam McLean.
4   Money was required to pay for the new stand which was opened in 1929.
5   John, Bertie and Alec.
6   Motherwell won the Scottish League in 1932.
7   John McMenemy.
8   Jimmy Delaney.
9   Jimmy Delaney.
10 Sunderland and Hearts.
11 Johnny Crum.
12 Clyde.

Disasters

4

1 Celtic lost the Scottish Cup final replay 0–3 to Rangers. It was the night of the infamous Hampden walk out.
2 Tommy Gemmell.
3 Celtic had sold Kenny Dalglish to Liverpool a few days earlier.
4 Du Wei and Roy Keane.
5 St Mirren.
6 Rangers 8 Celtic 1.
7 High winds and the fear of bits of Celtic Park's stands being blown off onto the crowd.
8 It was the Scottish Cup final of 1955 when Celtic and Clyde drew 1–1. Unhappily Celtic lost a late goal scored direct from a corner kick and involving a goalkeeping error.
9 Uruguay.
10 Celtic 0 Aberdeen 0.
11 Joe Craig.
12 Third Lanark.

Europe

1 Valencia.
2 Vojvodina Novi Sad.
3 Leeds United, Blackburn Rovers and Liverpool.
4 Dixie Deans.
5 1964.
6 George McCluskey and Johnny Doyle.
7 Kenny Dalglish and Henrik Larsson.
8 Paul Lambert.
9 Fiorentina.
10 Basel.
11 Aiden McGeady.
12 Liam Brady.

Foreign Players

1 John Hartson, Craig Bellamy and Joe Ledley.
2 Bulgarian.
3 James 'Joe' Kennaway.
4 Bent Martin.
5 Johannes Edvaldsson.
6 Joos Valgaeren played for Celtic in the Scottish League Cup final against Kilmarnock of 18 March 2001, then for Belgium against Scotland on 24 March 2001.
7 Brazilian.
8 Didier Agathe.
9 Emilio Izaguirre.
10 Efe Ambrose.
11 Leeds United, Middlesbrough and Newcastle United.
12 Israeli.

Founding Fathers

1 Sergeant Thomas Maley deliberately allowed Patrick Welsh, suspected of Fenian activities in 1867, to escape onto a ship about to sail from Dublin to Glasgow.
2 His brother, Tom.
3 He only had one arm.
4 He suggested that they light some candles.
5 James Kelly.
6 Hibs and Cowlairs.
7 Dundee Harp.
8 Neil McCallum.
9 John H. McLaughlin.
10 1893.
11 Johnny Madden.
12 Sandy McMahon.

Henrik Larsson

1 Feyenoord.
2 Hibs.
3 Scottish League Cup against Dundee United on 30 November 1997.
4 He broke his leg in a UEFA Cup game in Lyon.
5 53.
6 Kilmarnock.
7 She is his wife.
8 Livingston.
9 Stiliyan Petrov.
10 Arsenal.
11 106.
12 Manchester United.

Irish Players

1 Roy Keane.
2 Patsy Gallacher.
3 Allen McKnight.
4 Cornwall.
5 Willie Maley, Liam Brady, Martin O'Neill and Neil Lennon.
6 Charlie Tully.
7 Willie Cook.
8 Bertie Peacock.
9 Charlie Gallagher.
10 Centre forward.
11 He was Jock Stein's last signing.
12 Arsenal, Blackburn Rovers, Millwall and Bristol Rovers.

Jimmy McGrory

1 St Roch's.
2 Clydebank.
3 'Jean' McFarlane.
4 Tommy McInally.
5 Bob McPhail.
6 Motherwell.
7 In the course of it he equalled and then broke Steve Bloomer's record tally of goals.
8 3 minutes.
9 50.
10 Kilmarnock.
11 1945.
12 1954.

Jimmy Quinn

1 Croy.
2 Smithston Albion.
3 Left-winger.
4 Either the British League Cup or the Coronation Cup or the Exhibition Cup.
5 It was the first ever Cup final played at the new Hampden Park.
6 Alec Craig.
7 Shoulder charging. It means that as long as the goalkeeper has his feet on the ground, and the ball in his arms, he can be bundled into the net by a shoulder (not an elbow) charge.
8 Dublin.
9 11.
10 5.
11 1915.
12 His son John was killed in Holland while serving with the Argyll and Sutherland Highlanders.

Round 12 **Jock Stein**

1 1922.
2 Llanelli.
3 The Coronation Cup.
4 Bobbie Evans and Bertie Peacock.
5 Dunfermline Athletic, managed by Stein, beat Celtic 2–0 in the final of the Scottish Cup.
6 Hibs.
7 Ten.
8 1969.
9 Joe McBride and Dixie Deans.
10 Fans.
11 Leeds United.
12 He collapsed and died on 10 September 1985 at full time when managing Scotland against Wales in a World Cup qualifier at Ninian Park, Cardiff.

Lisbon 1967

1 Thursday.
2 John Fallon.
3 To secure the favoured bench and prevent Helenio Herrera seizing it!
4 He started singing 'The Celtic Song'.
5 Bertie Auld (with Birmingham City in the Inter Cities Fairs Cup in 1961).
6 Twice.
7 Kenneth Wolstenholme.
8 Bobby Murdoch.
9 Jim Craig.
10 Luis Suarez.
11 Real Madrid.
12 Dynamo Kiev.

Long, Long Ago

1 Queen's Park.
2 The Glasgow Charity Cup (or to give its proper name –
   the Glasgow Merchants' Charity Cup).
3 Celtic's game against Hibs was delayed because three men
   (John Divers, Peter Meehan and Barney Battles) went on
   strike because of comments made about them in the press!
4 Dundee.
5 Doyle and McArthur.
6 Jim Welford.
7 Ibrox was out of action because of the Ibrox disaster of
   three weeks previously, and Hampden was not yet built.
8 Celtic wore the horizontal green and white stripes for the
   first time.
9 It was the day of Queen Victoria's funeral.
10 Paddy Travers.
11 Davie McLean.
12 Burnley.

Round 15 Managers

1 Alloa Athletic and Hamilton Academical.
2 Once in 1954.
3 Kilmarnock.
4 He played for Feyenoord in the 1970 European Cup final.
5 Frank Connor.
6 Frank McGarvey.
7 Rangers.
8 St Mirren.
9 Aston Villa.
10 Kenny Dalglish.
11 Dundee.
12 Albion Rovers.

Round 16 Nicknames

1 Johannes Edvaldsson.
2 Alec Bennett.
3 Ronnie Simpson.
4 Forfar Athletic.
5 Jock Stein.
6 Napoleon.
7 Charlie Napier.
8 Ian Ure.
9 After Cesar (or Caesar) Romero, the actor, and perhaps also after Julius Caesar because he was such a powerful leader.
10 John Clark.
11 Sunny Jim.
12 Jimmy Johnstone.

Opponents

1   Dundee United.
2   Stark's Park, Kirkcaldy, home of Raith Rovers.
3   Annan Athletic.
4   Clyde.
5   Third Lanark in 1889.
6   Queen's Park.
7   Leith Athletic.
8   St Johnstone.
9   Whitehill Welfare.
10 Hearts and Dunfermline Athletic.
11 Rangers lost to Aberdeen at Ibrox and, barring some
    impossible score in Celtic's last game at Dunfermline,
    Celtic would be the champions.
12 Lochgelly United in 1923 and Burntisland in 1939.

Patsy Gallacher

 1 Donegal.
 2 1911.
 3 Four.
 4 Jimmy 'Napoleon' McMenemy had to move to inside left to accommodate him.
 5 He was guilty of 'bad timekeeping' in his wartime day job at John Brown's shipyard.
 6 He was playing for Ireland against Scotland.
 7 Rangers.
 8 A publican or a wine and spirits merchant.
 9 Falkirk.
10 'Will ye no' come back again?' This was because he was now playing for Falkirk, and they felt that Celtic released him prematurely.
11 John Divers.
12 Dundee.

Round 19   **Pictures**

1   The Glasgow Charity Cup, the Scottish Cup and the Glasgow Cup.
2   Middle row, fourth from the left.
3   Middle row, extreme left.
4   Middle row, third from the left.
5   Front row, second from the right.
6   Jock Stein and Charlie Tully.
7   Aberdeen.
8   Willie Wallace.
9   The Scottish Cup final of 1967.
10   Dundee United.
11   It is 5 September 1931 and the fatally injured John Thomson is being lifted into the ambulance outside Ibrox Park.
12   Jimmy Delaney.

Quotes

1 Jock Stein.
2 Willie Maley.
3 Dixie Deans.
4 Jimmy Johnstone.
5 Brother Walfrid, but also attributed to Willie Maley.
6 Jock Stein.
7 Sunny Jim Young, but also attributed to Jimmy McStay.
8 Fergus McCann.
9 Neil Lennon.
10 Pierre Van Hooijdonk.
11 Bill Shankly.
12 Either Dan Doyle or Sandy McMahon.

Records

1 Alec McNair.
2 Bobby Lennox.
3 Dunfermline Athletic.
4 Leeds United in 1970.
5 Aberdeen.
6 Motherwell.
7 Pat Bonner with 80 for the Republic of Ireland.
8 They beat Aberdeen 9–0.
9 They went 66 games without a single defeat.
10 In the European Cup semi-final against Inter Milan on 19 April 1972.
11 1938.
12 Cappielow, the home of Greenock Morton.

Scottish Cup

1 Five times – 1892, 1900, 1911, 1912 and 1914.
2 Willie Wallace.
3 Seven times – 1899, 1904, 1969, 1971, 1977, 1980 and 1989.
4 St Mirren.
5 Chris Sutton.
6 Joe Cassidy.
7 1980.
8 1909.
9 Bobby Murdoch.
10 2000 and 2003.
11 He was sent off.
12 Clydebank.

Round 23 — Scottish League Cup

1. Billy Simpson.
2. Partick Thistle.
3. East Fife.
4. Billy McPhail, Bobby Lennox, Dixie Deans and Henrik Larsson.
5. A fire at Hampden.
6. Partick Thistle, Hibs, Dundee and Aberdeen.
7. Chris Sutton.
8. Dion Dublin.
9. John Hughes.
10. Airdrie.
11. Dundee United in season 1997/98.
12. Hearts.

Scottish League

Round 24

1 1893.
2 Celtic beat Rangers 2–1 at Hampden in a play-off, the two teams having finished on equal points.
3 Bayview.
4 Scott McDonald.
5 Hibs.
6 Dundee.
7 He scored twice for Dundee to beat Hearts 2–0 at Dens Park while Celtic were beating St Mirren 5–0.
8 Joe Kennaway.
9 Dens Park.
10 40 years old.
11 Dundee.
12 Hearts.

Songs and Singers

1 1961.
2 McGrory.
3 Frank Haffey.
4 John Divers.
5 Kilmacolm.
6 Wellesley.
7 The Coronation Cup of 1953.
8 Rod Stewart.
9 It was the day after the end of the General Strike, and Celtic supporters were expressing their hatred of some of the Queen's Park players who had been involved in strike-breaking activities.
10 Lev Yashin.
11 No Defenders!
12 The King of Kings.

| | | |

Round 26 — Strange But True

1 Neil Mochan was signed in April 1953 and won the Glasgow Charity Cup and Coronation Cup, all played at grounds other than Celtic Park.
2 John Divers.
3 John Kennedy against Romania in 2004.
4 Joe Craig against Sweden in 1977.
5 Derry City.
6 This victory gave the Scottish League to Rangers who that same afternoon lost to Aberdeen at Ibrox and thought they had thrown away the League.
7 A Uruguayan policeman with a sword!
8 Three separate players (Bobby Murdoch, Harry Hood and Kenny Dalglish) all missed penalties!
9 He scored 2 own goals in the latter stages of the game, which Celtic lost 0–3.
10 A rabbit ran on the field.
11 He kicked a ball into the face of referee Mr Cuthill of Edinburgh. It was a pure accident, but after treatment, the referee, still stunned, sent Doyle off!
12 One of the girls entertaining the crowd at half-time responded to chants of 'get them off' by doing just that and removing her top. Naturally, your writer averted his gaze.

Round 27 | The Dear Old Paradise

1 1892.
2 Hampden Park had now been built and it was a lot bigger than Celtic Park.
3 The 'Jungle'.
4 1966.
5 The steam from everyone breathing prevented a good view!
6 The war disabled and the blind.
7 Clergymen (of all denominations).
8 1959.
9 West.
10 None!
11 1993 (Rangers beat Aberdeen) and 1998 (Hearts beat Rangers).
12 Litter! The two end stands had not yet been built, and there was nothing there to break the very strong west wind.

Wartime

1 Hearts.
2 They had to play 2 games on the same day against Raith Rovers at Parkhead and Motherwell at Fir Park. They won them both and in doing so won the League!
3 Peter Johnstone.
4 The sinking of the *Lusitania*.
5 Jimmy McColl.
6 Willie Lyon.
7 He was still recovering from his shattered arm sustained on 1 April 1939.
8 He scored the only goal in the Glasgow Cup final against Rangers at Ibrox.
9 Matt Busby.
10 Third Lanark.
11 Willie Miller.
12 The game finished as a 1–1 draw, and the issue was decided on corners so Celtic won 3–2.

Who Am I?

1 Davie Provan.
2 Peter Scarff.
3 Lubomir Moravcik.
4 Bobby Collins.
5 Jimmy McMenemy.
6 Bobby Murdoch.
7 Roddie MacDonald.
8 Paul McStay.
9 Martin O'Neill.
10 Maurice Johnston.
11 Charlie Nicholas.
12 Bertie Auld.

Willie Maley

1 A soldier in the British Army in Ireland.
2 Helen Pye.
3 Right half.
4 This was his mother's maiden name, and he did not want his employers to know that he played part-time professional football on a Saturday, so for the benefit of the press, he became 'Willie Montgomery'.
5 Arthurlie.
6 Twice.
7 Athletics and cycling.
8 Tommy McInally.
9 14.
10 William Wilton.
11 Jimmy McMenemy.
12 1958.

If you enjoyed this book, you may also be interested in …

The Celtic FC Miscellany

DAVID POTTER

Celtic inspires strong feelings in almost everyone. It is of course virtually impossible to chronicle all that has happened in the history of the club, but this little gem draws together some of the most interesting, quirky and downright odd events that have taken place over their long and auspicious existence. Packed with facts, stats, trivia, stories and legend, the reader will delve deep to find out all about the events and people who have shaped the club into what it is today.

978 0 7524 6462 6

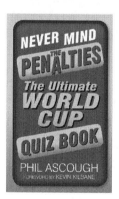

Never Mind the Penalties

PHIL ASCOUGH

England haven't won it since 1966 but every time the World Cup is played, there's always hope that this year will be *the* year. The World Cup has its critics but time stands still when your team plays. *Never Mind the Penalties* is the ultimate collection of World Cup teasers, pulling together the highs and lows, the bizarre and the beautiful from football's greatest tournament. Test your mates in the pub or liven up the pre-match warm-up – it's an essential part of your World Cup build-up.

978 0 7509 5842 4

Printed in Poland
by Amazon Fulfillment
Poland Sp. z o.o., Wrocław

51696538R00074